J.K. ROWLING'S
# Wizarding World™

# Movie
# MAGIC

✦ VOLUME 3 ✦

J.K. ROWLING'S
Wizarding World™

# Movie
# MAGIC

VOLUME 3

## Amazing Artifacts

Bonnie Burton

CANDLEWICK
PRESS

*An Insight Editions Book*

# CONTENTS

# Introduction

Many of the magical objects in J.K. Rowling's Wizarding World—from wands and racing brooms to Horcruxes, the Deathly Hallows, and Newt Scamander's case—are artifacts that were carefully designed and produced for the movies. Bringing these items from the written page to life on the movie screen involves its own version of wizardry and is accomplished by talented teams of concept artists, graphic designers, visual effects artists, and prop makers who work together with the production designer, director, and producers.

### Production Designer

The production designer helps decide how the environments—and everything in them—will look in a film. Production designers also guide the concept artists, visual effects artists, graphic designers, prop makers, model makers, and others in the art department to make sure they understand the overall look and feel of the film. Stuart Craig is the talented production designer responsible for all of the Harry Potter films as well as *Fantastic Beasts and Where to Find Them*.

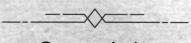

### Concept Artist

Concept artists visualize what props, environments, and characters will look like in a film. They create sketches and illustrations of people, places, and things so that the production designer, visual effects supervisors, directors, and producers can choose from different options before deciding on what to construct and build for the film.

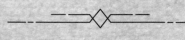

### Graphic Designer

Graphic designers create the printed items seen in the films, such as wanted posters, spell book covers, store signs, and food product labels. Miraphora Mina and Eduardo Lima and their team were the graphic designers responsible for the Harry Potter films and *Fantastic Beasts and Where to Find Them*. Together they created a variety of props, including newspapers, journals, speakeasy posters, and even all the vial labels found in the Hogwarts Potions classrooms and inside Newt Scamander's shed.

## Prop Maker

Prop makers build and construct objects to use in movies for practical effects—as opposed to computer-generated props. They build everything from personalized wands to the Magical Exposure Threat-Level Barometer in *Fantastic Beasts and Where to Find Them*. Prop makers also build durable stunt versions of wands and brooms for actors to use in action scenes. For the Harry Potter films, prop maker Pierre Bohanna created an unusual array of magical artifacts, including the Triwizard Tournament Cup, wands, and Albus Dumbledore's Memory Cabinet.

## Visual Effects Artist

Visual effects artists create artifacts digitally. They often add the magical properties to artifacts, such as making wands glow, brooms fly, and giant chess pieces move by themselves. *Fantastic Beasts and Where to Find Them* visual effects supervisors Tim Burke and Christian Manz helped to make all the complex creature environments inside Newt Scamander's case look believable, while the Harry Potter visual effects supervisor, John Richardson, helped everything from Hogwarts acceptance letters to the Weasley family car take flight.

---◇---

## Set Decorator

Set decorators make props and artifacts look right at home in their magical environments. They collaborate with production designers and directors by using art, props, furniture, and other details to design rooms. Harry Potter set decorator Stephanie McMillan stocked the Hogwarts library with lightweight books so they could be easily manipulated to look like they jumped off the shelves at students in *Harry Potter and the Half-Blood Prince*.

PART I

# FANTASTIC BEASTS
### AND WHERE TO FIND THEM

# NEWT SCAMANDER'S MAGICAL CASE

When Newt Scamander steps off the boat in New York City, he carries with him what appears to be an ordinary leather case. In fact, when the customs agent asks to take a look inside the case, all he finds are some harmless and common items: a New York City map, a magnifying glass, binoculars, an alarm clock, and folded clothes. The only item related to the wizarding world is a scarf bearing the black-and-yellow pattern associated with Hogwarts's Hufflepuff house. But there's much more to Newt's case than meets the eye.

## The World Within

Newt's leather case is actually bewitched with an Undetectable Extension Charm, making it large enough to contain a shed *and* a whole slew of fantastic beasts. There is so much space inside Newt's case that he is able to house everything from tiny insects like Billywigs to an enormous creature like the Erumpent. So how does Newt keep all this a secret from the No-Maj (non-magic) world? The case comes equipped with a switch to make it "Muggleworthy," enchanting it so that No-Majs (or Muggles, as British wizards would say) can't see or gain access to the creatures hidden inside.

# CREATURE COMFORTS

You can imagine that traveling around inside a leather case—even one with an Undetectable Extension Charm—might get a bit cramped for wild beasts. Newt has saved many of these creatures from danger or mistreatment, so making sure they are as safe and content as possible is definitely a priority. With that said, a burrow-loving Niffler has different wants and needs from a moon-loving Mooncalf. Newt accommodates them all by giving each creature its own special habitat in the case. "There is a sort of wondrous plethora of terrains for them in the case," notes actor Eddie Redmayne (Newt Scamander). By dividing up his case into various habitats, Newt allows each creature to feel much more at home.

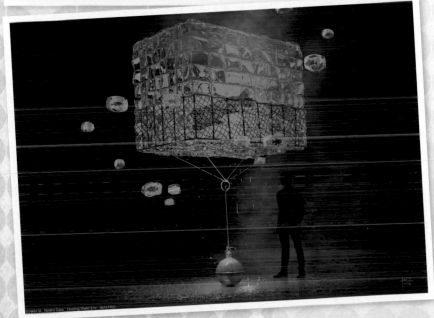

## An Infinite Diorama

The creature habitats are spectacularly different from one another. "There's an icy, arctic wasteland; a swampy area filled with mangroves; an area modeled after an Arizona desert; and a floating, rock-filled planet for the Mooncalves, among others," says production designer Stuart Craig, who worked with the visual effects team to bring the inside of Newt's case to life. One of the challenges for the filmmakers was figuring out exactly where one habitat would end and another begin. An early design made each habitat its own seemingly infinite environment. "It was a sort of magical world that initially appeared contained within a diorama that you could step into. Once you stepped into it, you became aware that you were actually in an expansive space, like the African savanna," says Stuart Craig.

## Simpler Magic

J.K. Rowling felt that the filmmaker's early idea for the habitats was maybe too advanced for Newt Scamander to accomplish. Even though Newt *is* a skilled wizard, it was important that the habitats looked like something Newt made on his own, using his own magic, and reflecting some of his own quirks and personality. So rather than the Thunderbird having its own infinite-seeming desert, it has a smaller space, but with a backdrop made to look like a desert.

## The Aquarium

Seen only briefly, the Grindylow's habitat is quite peculiar. Instead of building an aquarium, Newt has opted to use his magic to keep the water in a floating block, complete with a net. However, without walls to keep them in, it's easy for a fish or Grindylow to quickly find itself hovering in air!

# How to Enter a Magical Case

Entering the magical world inside of Newt's case is a thrilling experience for No-Maj Jacob Kowalski and for witches Tina and Queenie Goldstein. But figuring out just how a person would enter the case—and how a fantastic beast could be recaptured—was a bit of a challenge for the film's creative team.

## Mechanized Entry?

One of the first decisions that had to be made was whether entering the case would be more of a magical process or a mechanical one. One option showed how Newt and his guests would open the case and then step down into an old-fashioned elevator that would be loud and clattering as it moved downward. Another option showed the case propelling itself using magical clockwork. Yet another idea was that Newt would be swallowed into the case in a similar way to how wizards Apparate. After discussing each possibility, the filmmakers ultimately decided that they were overthinking the issue. That's why in the film, Newt just . . . steps down into his case!

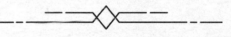

## Creature Capture

The case needed a way to prevent beasts from escaping and a way for Newt to recapture his beasts throughout the film, so the creative team came up with a variety of possible solutions. One idea was for Newt to treat the case like a bullfighter's cape in a bullfight: when Newt would hold out the case, the creature would be attracted to it, run toward it, and then disappear inside. Another idea was that the case could trap creatures larger than itself, but would take a while to gobble them up—like how a snake takes a while to swallow its prey.

# NEWT'S SHED

Newt Scamander is a Magizoologist—a person who studies magical creatures—and at the center of his case is his shed. Newt has been traveling the world alone for quite a while, so the filmmakers needed to make sure that everything Newt could possibly need to study and care for his magical creatures was right there. Newt is also a bit of a collector, and inside his shed there are journals, books, charts, vials, potion bottles, souvenirs, boxes of Billywig stings, and various other items on all of the slightly disheveled shelves and in the overfilled cabinet drawers.

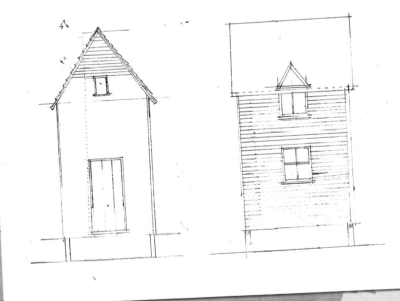

## A Whimsical Design

"Newt is a very independent character," production designer Stuart Craig says. "Being solitary seems to be a necessary part of his life at times; so we gave him a shed." Newt's utility shed is the entrance to the case's magical world. Concept artist Dermot Power based one of his original designs for Newt's thin but tall shed on the weather-beaten seaside huts you might see along the English coast, including wooden supports for the shed that were a little too thin—giving the whole structure a whimsical and flexible feel.

# Items a Magizoologist Needs: Newt's Artifacts

Newt keeps a variety of useful potions, balms, and ingredients needed to care for his creatures, including such items as Hoof Healer Ointment, Shell Shiner, Healthy Horn Polish, and Beak Balm. The film's graphics department created labels for each item and even included warnings, directions for use, and ingredients. Feather Floss, for example, is a useful ointment for mending injured Diricawl or Fwooper feathers, and Shell Shiner is made from dittany, wormwood, and salt water.

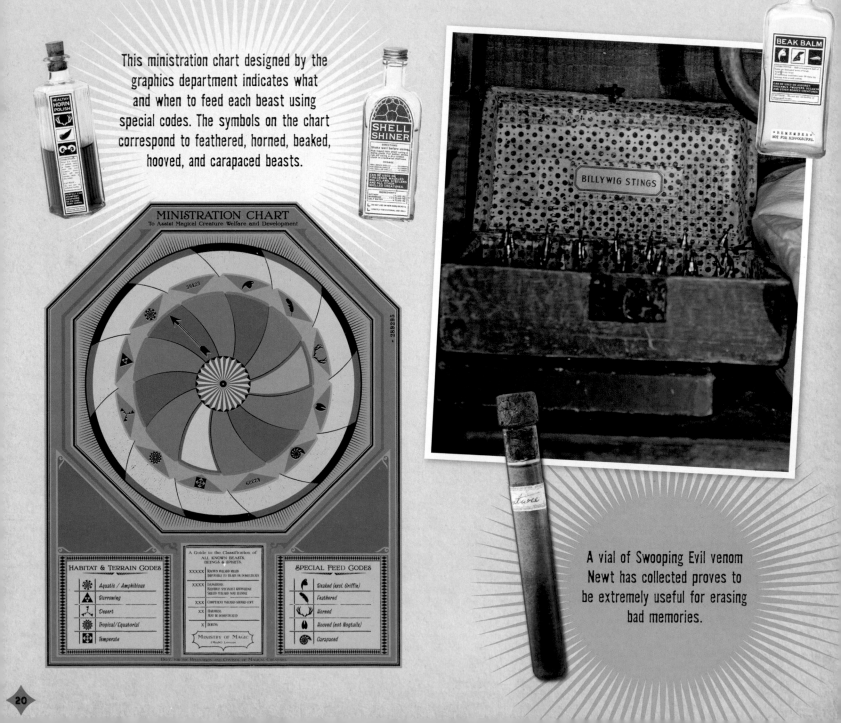

This ministration chart designed by the graphics department indicates what and when to feed each beast using special codes. The symbols on the chart correspond to feathered, horned, beaked, hooved, and carapaced beasts.

A vial of Swooping Evil venom Newt has collected proves to be extremely useful for erasing bad memories.

**Niffler**

*Should never be kept in a house.*

*Runs very fast.*

*Long fingers for grasping.*

Shaft

quill

TOP

*pouch used to store treasure.*

**HABITAT & TERRAIN CODES**

| | | |
|---|---|---|
| NO | | Aquatic / Amphibious |
| YES | | Burrowing ✓ |
| YES | | Forest |
| NO | | Tropical / Equatorial |
| NO | | Temperate |

## *tastic Beasts and Where to Find Them*

...t has just spent a year traveling the world
...earching and writing a book all about magical
...tures. The manuscript for what will become his
...me *Fantastic Beasts and Where to Find Them* is
...tained within a well-worn, marbled green folder
...h the logo of his publisher, Obscurus Books, on
...cover. The graphics team made sure to stuff
...volume with typed pages and quick sketches.
...Rowling asked that the graphics team prepare
...ther important book—the *Bestiarium Magicum*.
...a book about magical creatures from medieval
...es, which desperately needs updating. Newt's
...y would be well loved, since he'd likely have dug
...it for reference countless times.

### Notes from the Field

...ide from his manuscript, Newt also has several
...ebooks filled with the raw data and creature
...servations he's collected while abroad. Each
...rnal is embossed with his monogram.

## Newt's Wand

Since Newt dedicates his life to magical creatures, his wand had to have some sort of animal or natural component in its design and materials. But actor Eddie Redmayne, who plays Newt in the film, insisted that the wand not be made from animal bone, horn, or leather. Given Newt's love for his beasts, he wouldn't approve of his wand including some kind of creature trophy. Instead, Eddie chose a simple wand made of organic materials. The wand's handle appears to be made from a piece of shell, while the tip is made of ash wood.

Newt's wand has many nicks and scratches, giving it the look of a well-used but also beloved tool.

## Lunascope

A lunascope is a magical astronomical instrument that shows the phases of the moon. The lunascope is first seen on film in *Fantastic Beasts and Where to Find Them* when Newt offers one to Gnarlak in hopes of getting information about his missing creatures.

## Practically Portable

Although the lunascope is only briefly seen in the film, concept artist Molly Sole and prop makers still had to figure out what exactly it would look like. A tool to be used for determining exactly what phase the moon is in—essential to witches and wizards for getting the right dates for relevant spells, harvests, and rituals—it needed to be handy and more portable than carrying around a bunch of detailed moon charts.

In the end, the design ended up being a mash-up between a telescope and a sundial, with the idea being that the user would slide dials to find the relative distances between the moon, the North Star, and specific constellations—thus giving accurate measures of the current moon phase and predicting coming ones.

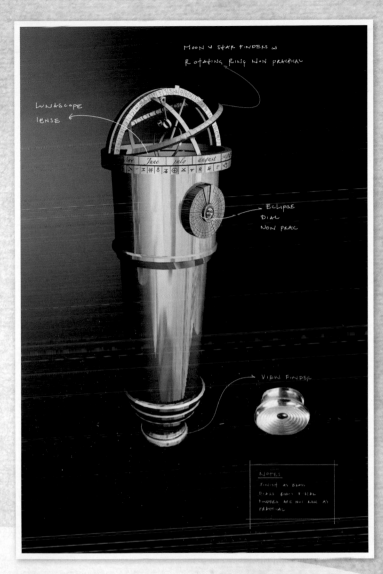

When Newt tries to bribe Gnarlak for information with a lunascope, Gnarlak only pretends to be interested. "I got five," he says. It's Pickett the Bowtruckle that catches Gnarlak's eye.

# Tina Goldstein's Artifacts

Tina Goldstein used to be an Auror, a highly trained witch or wizard charged with investigating crimes committed against the wizarding community. Recently demoted to a position at the Wand Permit Office at MACUSA for using unauthorized magic, Tina hasn't given up hope of regaining her old job. While keeping an eye on an anti-magic group, Tina comes across a wizard, Newt Scamander, who seems to be the cause of a disturbance at the City Bank. Even though it's no longer her job, she knows she's got to bring him in.

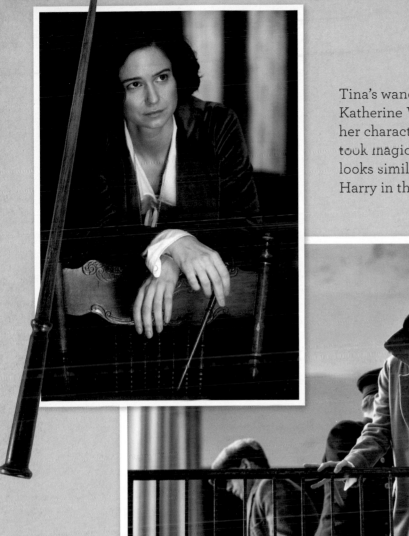

## Tina's Wand

Tina's wand is functional and understated. Actress Katherine Waterston, who plays Tina, requested that her character's wand have some heft to signify that she took magic very seriously. The uncomplicated wand looks similar to the design of the wand prop used by Harry in the first two Harry Potter films.

## MACUSA Identity Card

Perhaps an old habit from her Auror days, one of the first things Tina does when she meets Newt is flash her ID. Designed and filled in by hand by the graphics department, this card is used by MACUSA employees and contains a photograph; basic info such as height, weight, and date of birth; a set of fingerprints; and the owner's signature. Tina's ID card reveals that her full name is Porpentina Esther Goldstein, she is twenty-five, and her job title is "Federal Wand Permit Officer."

# QUEENIE GOLDSTEIN'S ARTIFACTS

Queenie is quite different from Tina. She is quirky, fashionable, and free-spirited; she doesn't have the same ambition as her big sister. One thing they do have in common is their dislike of working at the Wand Permit Office at MACUSA. She has a habit of faking being sick and using her charm on her boss, Mr. Abernathy, to get out of work early.

## She Likes to Cook!

Queenie loves to cook—if you can call it that! As Jacob notices when he has dinner at the Goldsteins' apartment, witches and wizards have quite a different way of preparing a meal, thanks to their magical powers. Queenie assembles a fantastic strudel in a jiffy. The graphics department made sure to fill out the Goldsteins' apartment with all kinds of useful items, creating graphics for self-charming flour, Elfin Sugar Crystals, and more.

## Glamour Products

Among the glamour and lifestyle magazines scattered about the Goldsteins' apartment are an assortment of WonderWitch products—the same brand seen at Weasleys' Wizard Wheezes in *Harry Potter and the Half-Blood Prince,* but outfitted by the graphics department with a retro design more appropriate to the era.

**FRANKS AND HUMAN BEANS**
*(Cook Like a No-Maj)*

RECIPES

*Carefully Tested for Time and Temperature*

For Jelly Making, Preserving, Baking, Roasting, Candy Making and Deep Fat Frying.

## Queenie's Wand

Unlike her sister Tina's ordinary-looking wand, Queenie's is ornate, reflecting her personality. Made from rosewood, the wand features a mother-of-pearl handle sculpted in the shape of a snail shell. Since actress Alison Sudol, who plays Queenie, loves all things art deco, the wand designers incorporated that preference into the design. The result is a glamorous wand that fits the chic witch perfectly.

## Queenie's Coat

Where Tina is gawky and serious, sister Queenie is light, fun, and trendsetting. The pink coat worn by Queenie was specially designed by costume designer Colleen Atwood and was woven from over five miles of thread.

# JACOB KOWALSKI'S ARTIFACTS

Jacob Kowalski is a No-Maj who works in a cannery but dreams of becoming a baker. Unable to secure a loan to open a bakery, Jacob seems resigned to his fate. But everything changes when he encounters Newt Scamander and is inadvertently swept up in the mayhem caused by Newt's magical beasts.

KOWALSKI

**K**

FANCY CONFECTIONS

443 RIVINGTON ST. NEW YORK.

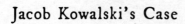

### Jacob Kowalski's Case

While Jacob's case looks a lot like Newt's case on the outside, it holds very different contents. Newt's case contains vast environments and creatures, while Jacob's contains something *almost* as magical—tasty pastries. Jacob brought his case of treats to the bank in an attempt to secure a loan to start his own bakery, but his application was rejected, and Jacob mistakenly grabs Newt's magical case.

## Occamy Egg

Due to its extremely valuable eggs, whose shells are pure silver, the Occamy is an endangered creature. Jacob receives some Occamy eggshells from an anonymous benefactor as collateral to start his bakery. For the film, the Occamy egg was designed to look like a palm-size duck egg with a weathered, organic feel, and features a silvery blue color that evokes the plumage of an adult Occamy.

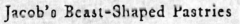

## Jacob's Beast-Shaped Pastries

Having secured a loan, Jacob finally opens his own bakery. He bakes treats in the shapes of Newt's fantastic beasts, which prove to be very popular with his customers. Among the regular loaves of bread on his shelves is a special display with an Erumpent loaf, a pączki Niffler, a pretzel Occamy, and an iced Demiguise that resembles a babka. Concept artist Molly Sole kept in mind Jacob's heritage, thus the pączki (a kind of doughnut) and the babka (a sweet, marbled cake), which are traditional Polish pastries.

# PERCIVAL GRAVES'S ARTIFACTS

MACUSA's Director of Magical Security Percival Graves is not what he seems. While he is very interested in Newt and his case of beasts, it becomes clear that his hidden agenda could be much more dangerous than Newt could have anticipated.

### Graves's Wand

Graves's wand is ebony with a silver band dividing the main tip and the handle in a simple art deco style. The handle also has a rear tip "almost like a walking stick," prop maker Pierre Bohanna says. The wand's design was inspired by an antique conductor's baton.

## The Deathly Hallows

Percival Graves hands over a Deathly Hallows pendant necklace to Credence Barebone to strengthen his will to help him find the Obscurus, and for Credence to signal Graves by touching it once he's located the Obscurial. The pendant appears to be of the same design as the one worn by Xenophilius Lovegood in *Harry Potter and the Deathly Hallows – Part 1*.

Graves wears a pair of ominous shirt collar pins that resemble scorpions.

# MAGICAL CONGRESS OF THE UNITED STATES OF AMERICA

The Magical Congress of the United States of America (MACUSA) was created to govern American wizards and witches. Headquartered at the Woolworth Building, a skyscraper in Lower Manhattan and the tallest building in the world in 1926, MACUSA is a sight to behold. Visitors step into a golden atrium with a spectacular, 750-foot-high ceiling. Inside the rooms of MACUSA, all kinds of wizarding activities take place, from the menial task of sorting wand permits to the execution of Dark wizards.

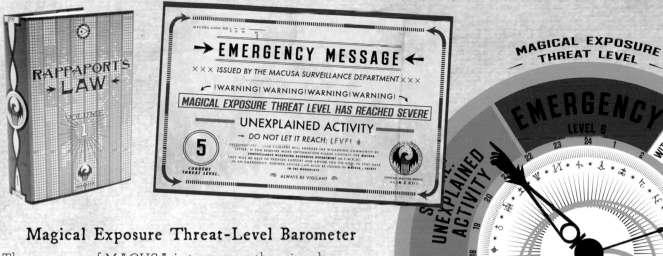

## Magical Exposure Threat-Level Barometer

The purpose of MACUSA is to govern the wizard community and keep it secret from No-Majs. To aid in its mission, the MACUSA building is equipped with a special barometer made by the Department for Magical Security that measures magical exposure to No-Maj citizens. When the face reads "SEVERE: UNEXPLAINED ACTIVITY," like it does when Newt and Tina first arrive at MACUSA, you know there is trouble. The enormous mechanical piece that hangs in the center atrium took the prop-making team six weeks to construct, and is complete with moving cogs.

The button layout seen in the MACUSA elevator is mysteriously missing a few floors.

### Going Up!

To get from floor to floor at MACUSA, employees and visitors will find themselves using the building's impressive elevator operated by Red. The goblin was designed by concept artists to look gruff and somewhat cantankerous. A bit short for an elevator operator, he uses a bejeweled stick to poke the elevator buttons for each floor.

# MACUSA Paperwork

Like at many government organizations, working at MACUSA involves filling out plenty of paperwork. The graphics team designed and printed thousands of items, from wand-permit applications to emergency memos and public-safety guidelines, ensuring that the wizarding government stacks up next to its Muggle counterpart in terms of documents.

Not all the documents seen are official. Just like in any office, there are plenty of goofy notes posted on bulletin boards by Queenie and Tina's coworkers.

ISSUED BY THE MACUSA SURVEILLANCE DEPARTMENT

## ALWAYS BE VIGILANT

OFFICIAL MACUSA MEMO
xx [M.S.0] xx

WARNING! WARNING! WARNING!
MAGICAL EXPOSURE THREAT LEVEL HAS REACHED SEVERE

You don't have to be
MAGIC
to work here...

☞ Actually YOU DO!

YOU CURSE IT,
YOU CURE IT!

## Do You Have a Permit for That?

Every American and visiting witch or wizard must fill [in] a permit application if they want to legally possess [and] use a wand. Information such as name, address, [MA]CUSA Identification Number or Alien Registration [Nu]mber, profession, U.S. address, and Owl Mail [Cod]e is required. The form also includes spaces for [dim]ensions, shape, type of wand wood, and most [rece]nt spells cast. The applications are then processed [by t]he Wand Permit Office—that's Tina and Queenie's [job.] In order to dress the Wand Permit Office set, the [grap]hics team printed 4,000 envelopes and affixed [them] with wax seals.

## Memorandum Rodentium

[At th]e Ministry of Magic, some memos fly, but at MACUSA, they scurry. In the [dark] depths of the MACUSA basement sits an enormous, deserted room where [self]-operating typewriters spit out documents in the form of origami rats. These ["Me]morandum Rodentium" can be seen dashing through a network of tubes to [th]eir destinations, or getting into arguments with one another. The cute rodents [we]re created through close collaboration among the graphics team, who drew them up originally, the props department, who built the prototype, and the visual effects department, who ultimately brought them to life on-screen.

---

### Form (left side)

FILE NO.
DEPARTMENT

MAGICAL CONGRESS OF THE UNITED STATES OF AMERICA

## APPLICATION FO[R]

**APPLICATION NUMBER**

APPLICANT'S LEGAL WIZARD NAME (FIRST)

APPLICANT'S LEGAL WIZARD NAME (MIDDLE)

APPLICANT'S LEGAL WIZARD NAME (SURNAME)

☐ MALE  ☐ FEMALE        /   /
SEX                    DATE OF BIRTH

M.A.C.U.S.A IDENTIFICATION NUMBER

IF ALIEN CITIZEN - INPUT YOUR ALIEN REGISTRATION NUMBER

PROFESSION

CURRENT USA RESIDENTIAL ADDRESS

CURRENT USA RESIDENTIAL ADDRESS

CITY / STATE        OWL MAIL CODE

## WAND INFORMATION

L        W        R

DIMENSIONS

DETAILED DESCRIPTION - DECORATION

DETAILED DESCRIPTION - SHAPE

DETAILED DESCRIPTION - COLOUR

## TYPE OF WOOD

| | | |
|---|---|---|
| ◯ Holly | ◯ Sycamore | ◯ Ebony |
| ◯ Hawthorn | ◯ Fir | ◯ Hazel |
| ◯ Pear | ◯ Oak | ◯ Cherry |
| ◯ Pine | ◯ Rowan | ◯ Cedar |
| ◯ Ivy | ◯ Rosewood | ◯ Blackthorn |
| ◯ Willow | ◯ Elm | ◯ Ash |
| ◯ Mahogany | ◯ Yew | ◯ Birch |
| ◯ Sugar Maple | ◯ Tamarack | |
| ◯ Aspen | | |

---

### Wand Permit tag (right side)

MACUSA

APPLICATION FOR WAND PERMIT

HAVE YOU REMEMBERED?
Remove all questions.
Sign the application.
Insert your wand
if asked to do so.
DO NOT FORGET
to close this by
using a
SEALANT
CHARM.

To:
WAND PERMIT
OFFICE, MACUSA

MANHATTAN,
NEW YORK CITY

CARRIAGE
BY OWL

# NEW SALEM PHILANTHROPIC SOCIETY

Members of the New Salem Philanthropic Society (N.S.P.S., or the Second Salemers) believe that wizards and witches are practicing magic in New York City and that they are behind some of the sinister incidents occurring there. The N.S.P.S. is led by Mary Lou Barebone, who holds anti-magic rallies with her three adopted children—Credence, Chastity, and Modesty—in tow. The ramshackle headquarters of the group is a neglected church in New York City's Lower East Side, where the N.S.P.S. prints and distributes flyers and posters.

### A Destructive Logo

A pair of hands breaking a wand in half is the symbol of the Second Salemers. In an early draft of the script, the symbol was described as being a broken wand with a dove, but the filmmakers ultimately decided they wanted a more aggressively anti-magic symbol. A wand being violently snapped in half amid flames was a perfect metaphor for Mary Lou's mission. The N.S.P.S. banner seen hanging in Second Salemers' headquarters was made from scratch using red velvet and a satin appliqué with embroidered embellishments.

### "Witches Live Among Us" Pamphlet

If they want their supper, the children who congregate at the New Salem Philanthropic Society church will need to pass out dozens of copies of this anti-witchcraft propaganda. Depicting a wild dance around a fire, this booklet highlights N.S.P.S.'s agenda to expose witches and wizards. In addition to the booklets, of which thousands were printed, the graphics team designed a number of different posters and signs for use by Second Salemers.

# THE BLIND PIG

The Blind Pig is a magical speakeasy and jazz club run by Gnarlak, an American goblin gangster. Located in New York City, its entrance is disguised by an enchanted poster of a beautiful woman advertising lipstick, which uses the catchphrases "Lips That Charm!" and "Enchanting. Beguiling. Alluring." When a wizard, witch, or other magical being approaches, the woman on the poster comes to life, and the brick wall disappears to reveal a door. "We based it on makeup ads from that time—the color palette, the font, the feel of it," explains graphic designer Eduardo Lima.

In 1926, the United States was in the middle of Prohibition—an era when transporting and selling alcohol was illegal. To accommodate those who refused to give up their cocktails, secret speakeasy clubs and bars popped up all over New York City and other cities around the country. Alcohol wasn't outlawed in the wizarding world, but The Blind Pig still has plenty of unregulated activity going on. Walk into The Blind Pig and you'll find wizards, witches, and magical beings as its thirsty patrons looking for an entertaining night out. In the film, Newt Scamander visits The Blind Pig with Tina, Queenie, and Jacob in search of information about his missing creatures.

## Drink Up if You Dare . . .

When patrons belly up to the bar, the elf bartender snaps his fingers to make bottles of alcohol float in midair as he mixes their drinks. The art department made the bottles of booze look extra-dangerous by adding skeletons and skulls to the labels. Other drinks had more high-class labels, like Dragon's Fire Whisky.

The special effects team added ominous effects to the drinks, including making them glow and billow smoke.

## It's in the Cards

The Blind Pig is part of the seedy underbelly of the wizarding world, so it's not surprising that there's some gambling going on at the establishment. Customers can be seen crouched over tables, gambling with dice for unusual but valuable artifacts. Wizards, witches, goblins, and giants alike all try their hand in a card game hoping Lady Luck will look favorably on them. Dice featuring wizarding runes were created for the set, along with a deck of cards featuring images from the magical world.

# All That Jazz!

Speakeasies weren't only known for strong cocktails and secret gambling; they were also places to hear great music. In the 1920s, the Jazz Age was in full swing, which meant every speakeasy had to have a talented band with a stunning singer wooing the crowd. The house band at The Blind Pig features a mix of humans and goblins (created via motion capture with real actors). In addition to the goblin crooner, the five-piece house band comprises a pianist, a drummer, a banjo player, a double bassist, and a sousaphone player. Each of the instruments was designed by concept artist Rob Bliss, then crafted by the prop-making team.

## Magical Music

Every instrument in the jazz band was given some kind of magical touch. Production designer Stuart Craig came up with the idea of an upright grand piano, for example, that would be left slightly open so you could see all the strings. The banjo at The Blind Pig has three different necks. The most extravagant setup went to the brass player, who had a dozen different types of brass and wind instruments floating around him, several of which he played at once. To make these pieces appear to float, they were mounted on blacked-out stands.

# MOST WANTED CUSTOMERS

The walls of The Blind Pig are decorated with numerous wanted posters that just so happen to feature some of the regulars. The wanted posters include different types of criminals, from the wanded and extremely dangerous to those wanted for money laundering, counterfeiting wands, or elf trafficking. The posters were designed and aged by the graphics team, but were enhanced with moving photographs thanks to the visual effects department. Actors were filmed in front of a green screen and added to the posters later.

It isn't long before the wanted posters at The Blind Pig are updated with MACUSA's latest escapees—Newt and Tina.

# BOOKS AND OTHER READING MATERIALS

You can tell a lot about a person from the kinds of books they own, and the wizarding world is no different. For example, Tina owns *Living with Legilimens*, a self-help book that coaches readers on how to live with someone who has the power to read minds. It's a useful read for someone with a Legilimens sister. Queenie, on the other hand, likes to keep up on the latest fashions with breezier periodicals like *The American Charmer* and *The Witch's Friend*. The books and other reading materials seen throughout *Fantastic Beasts and Where to Find Them* were designed with great attention to detail by the graphics department.

### Old Treasures

To craft the graphic elements for *Fantastic Beasts and Where to Find Them*, graphic artists Miraphora Mina and Eduardo Lima focused their research on unearthing ephemera from the 1850s through to the 1950s. It was important that every aspect of the designs created for the film felt grounded in reality to an extent, so everything from real-life business cards to photographs, posters, and more were referenced. From there, a bit of magic and wonder was worked into the designs. Throughout the process, the graphic designers who worked on the film thought about how best to tell the story through the often small, incidental pieces that are part of the background of the film.

### *The Intricacies of Rappaport's Law* and *Scourers and the Creation of MACUSA*

In part because of the Salem Witch Trials, the laws governing how magical and No-Maj people interact are very different in the United States and Newt's native England. Part of the graphics team's job was to make sure that wizarding America's fear of exposure was communicated in some of their designs and that there was a sense of the unique and troubled history of American witches and wizards.

Rappaport's Law was created to ensure complete segregation between the magical and No-Maj communities.

## The New York Ghost Newspaper

Playing on the name of the *New York Post*, one of America's oldest newspapers, this wizarding periodical is the U.S. equivalent to the *Daily Prophet*. In the film, *The New York Ghost* often reports about the deadly wizard Gellert Grindelwald evading capture, but the graphics department also had a bit of fun coming up with other happenings about town. Headlines call attention to Voodoo leniency, an herbologist being attacked by Mandrakes, healers demanding negotiations over working hours, and even Quidditch quizzes.

This seven-volume series of books is found in Tina and Queenie's brownstone apartment. It was required reading during their days at Ilvermorny School of Witchcraft and Wizardry.

Jacob Kowalski is reading this magical story in bed at Tina and Queenie Goldstein's apartment before Newt invites him into his case.

PART II

# Harry Potter™

# HOGWARTS ACCEPTANCE LETTER

Having their child accepted to Hogwarts School of Witchcraft and Wizardry should be a cause for celebration for a young witch or wizard's parents. Unfortunately for Harry Potter, his uncle, Vernon Dursley, doesn't see it that way. Uncle Vernon will try anything to stop Harry from reading his acceptance letter. In the end, ten thousand letters were delivered to the Dursleys' house at number four, Privet Drive before Harry was finally able to read his invitation to the school.

## Envelope Flingers

How do you fill a living room with ten thousand flying letters? While the filmmakers considered using computer-generated special effects, they were ultimately convinced to do the scene as a practical effect, using machines. Into the top of the set of the Dursleys' living room, machines were built that would fling the envelopes out at a very rapid but controlled speed. Another mechanism was even built to fire them down the chimney!

## Every Kind of Envelope

Different types of envelopes were used to flood the Dursleys' living room, including light ones to fly around the room and others with a real wax stamp of the Hogwarts seal for close-up shots. The wax-stamped envelopes held the acceptance letter, which was hand signed by graphic artist Miraphora Mina.

MR H. POTTER,
The Cupboard *under the* Stairs,
4, Privet Drive,
Little Whinging,
SURREY

FIRST YEAR
HOGWARTS SCHOOL
UNIFORM   EQUIPMENT   BOOK LIST
LIST

PRIVET DRIVE

HOGWARTS
DRACO DORMIENS NUNQUAM TITILLANDUS

To:   Mr Harry Potter
      The Cupboard Under the Stairs,
      4 Privet Drive,
      Little Whinging,
      SURREY.

...materials for first years.

"...equipped ...standard ...cauldron, and ...bring, if they desire, either an owl, a cat, or a toad."—Letter from Lucinda Thomsonicle-Pocus, Harry Potter and the Sorcerer's Stone.

HOGWARTS SCHOOL of WITCHCRAFT & WIZARDRY
Headmaster: Albus Dumbledore, D.Wiz., X.J.(sorc.), S.of Mag.Q.

# The Sorting Hat

For generations, the Sorting Hat has placed first-year witches and wizards into one of the four Hogwarts houses: Gryffindor, Slytherin, Ravenclaw, and Hufflepuff. Though only one Sorting Ceremony is seen on-screen, the Sorting Hat appears throughout the Harry Potter films, such as in Professor Dumbledore's office in *Harry Potter and the Chamber of Secrets* and during the Battle of Hogwarts in *Harry Potter and the Deathly Hallows – Part 2*.

### The Real Hat

The Sorting Hat prop was designed by costume designer Judianna Makovsky for *Harry Potter and the Sorcerer's Stone*. Over the course of the films, seven versions of the hat were created. Each hat was made out of suede and lined with horsehair canvas, dyed for color, and printed very faintly with Celtic symbols.

### Make It Talk!

Though Judianna Makovsky and her team made the Sorting Hat prop, it took another process entirely to make it speak! A computer-generated replica was used to sort the first years into their houses.

## Every Kind of Envelope

Different types of envelopes were used to flood the Dursleys' living room, including light ones to fly around the room and others with a real wax stamp of the Hogwarts seal for close-up shots. The wax-stamped envelopes held the acceptance letter, which was hand signed by graphic artist Miraphora Mina.

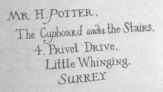

MR. H. POTTER,
The Cupboard under the Stairs,
4, Privet Drive,
Little Whinging,
SURREY

FIRST YEAR
**HOGWARTS SCHOOL**
UNIFORM · EQUIPMENT · BOOK LIST
**LIST**

FIRST YEAR STUDENTS WILL REQUIRE:

1. Three sets of plain ... robes
2. One plain pointed ha ... day wear
3. One pair of dragon-h ... ves

AND THE FOLLOWING SET BOOKS:

1. "The Standard Book of Spells" by Miranda Goshawk
2. "One Thousand Magical Herbs and Fungi" by Phyllida Spore
3. "A History of Magic" by Bathilda Bagshot
4. "Magical Theory" by Adalbert Waffling
5. "A Beginner's Guide to Transfiguration" by Emeric Switch
6. "Magical Drafts and Potions" by Arsenius Jigger
7. "Fantastic Beasts and where to find them" by Newt Scamander
8. "The Dark Forces: A Guide to Self-Protection" by Quentin Trimble

ALL STUDENTS MUST BE EQUIPPED WITH:

1. One Wand
2. One standard Size 2 pewter cauldron
...and may bring, if they desire, either an owl, a cat, or a toad.

Lucinda Thomsonicle~Pocus,
Chief Attendant of Witchcraft Provisions

**HOGWARTS SCHOOL of WITCHCRAFT & WIZARDRY**
Headmaster: Albus Dumbledore, D.Wiz., X.J.(sorc.), S.of Mag.Q.

## Owl Post

While some of the owls shown delivering envelopes to number four, Privet Drive were models or computer-generated, several were real. The real owls wore a special plastic harness that held the envelope to be delivered. A long, nearly invisible cord hung down from the harness: a trainer would tug at the cord at just the right moment to trigger the envelope to drop.

## Supply List

In addition to the acceptance letter, the graphics team also visualized the list of must-have school materials for first years.

"All students must be equipped with: one wand, one standard "Size 2" pewter cauldron, and may bring, if they desire, either an owl, a cat, or a toad."—Letter from Lucinda Thomsonicle—Pocus, Harry Potter and the Sorcerer's Stone.

# The Sorting Hat

For generations, the Sorting Hat has placed first-year witches and wizards into one of the four Hogwarts houses: Gryffindor, Slytherin, Ravenclaw, and Hufflepuff. Though only one Sorting Ceremony is seen on-screen, the Sorting Hat appears throughout the Harry Potter films, such as in Professor Dumbledore's office in *Harry Potter and the Chamber of Secrets* and during the Battle of Hogwarts in *Harry Potter and the Deathly Hallows – Part 2*.

### The Real Hat

The Sorting Hat prop was designed by costume designer Judianna Makovsky for *Harry Potter and the Sorcerer's Stone.* Over the course of the films, seven versions of the hat were created. Each hat was made out of suede and lined with horsehair canvas, dyed for color, and printed very faintly with Celtic symbols.

### Make It Talk!

Though Judianna Makovsky and her team made the Sorting Hat prop, it took another process entirely to make it speak! A computer-generated replica was used to sort the first years into their houses.

# THE SWORD OF GRYFFINDOR

A thousand-year-old artifact owned by Godric Gryffindor, the founder of Gryffindor house, this sword is goblin-made and enchanted with several magical qualities: it can be pulled from the Sorting Hat by a true Gryffindor in need, and the sword's special silver has the ability to take in substances that make it stronger. After Harry uses it to destroy the Basilisk in *Harry Potter and the Chamber of Secrets*, the sword absorbs the Basilisk's venom, which makes it a useful tool for destroying Horcruxes.

### Crafting the Blade

The prop-making team purchased a sword at an auction for reference and researched medieval swords for inspiration. The final prop is set with ruby-colored gems, which symbolize Gryffindor house, and is inscribed with Godric Gryffindor's name on the blade. There is also a small picture engraved on the handle of a wizard holding a scroll—perhaps intended to be Godric Gryffindor himself.

# BOOKS AND TEXTBOOKS

Hogwarts students are required to read a range of books for their studies, from *The Standard Book of Spells* by Miranda Goshawk to *A History of Magic* by Bathilda Bagshot and *Fantastic Beasts and Where to Find Them* by Newt Scamander. Designed by Miraphora Mina and Eduardo Lima, dozens of books were made for the Harry Potter films, though many are only seen on-screen for a moment, or not at all. Still, the designers put an enormous amount of care and attention into each and every prop, however small. The design of each one helped to convey the magic and mystery of the wizarding world.

## The Monster Book of Monsters

When Rubeus Hagrid becomes the Care of Magical Creatures professor at Hogwarts in *Harry Potter and the Prisoner of Azkaban,* he assigns his students *The Monster Book of Monsters* by Edwardus Lima. The unusual textbook looks like a monster itself, with a fur cover, multiple eyes, and very sharp teeth. Miraphora Mina designed multiple versions of the book, including one with a spiny tail and clawed feet. Another version used the red ribbon bookmark as the tongue.

Some of the books used as props had no authors, so the graphics department made them up. Miraphora Mina used her son's name for several of them.

A look inside *The Monster Book of Monsters* shows pages on house-elves and Mandrake roots.

# ADVANCED POTION-MAKING

Harry Potter isn't very good at Potions until he comes across a shabby-looking used copy of *Advanced Potion-Making*, marked up by the mysterious and talented "Half-Blood Prince." Two different versions of the textbook were designed by Miraphora Mina for *Harry Potter and the Half-Blood Prince*, and effort was made to make the new version look much more desirable, since Harry and Ron fight for it. The older version is well-worn, with Victorian-style lettering.

## Snape's Scribbles

To make all the handwritten notes in Harry's copy of *Advanced Potion-Making* look authentic, Miraphora Mina had to design Snape's signature scrawl. "Probably he wouldn't have it all tidy and in the same direction," says Miraphora, who made sure to show lots of thinking and scrubbing out.

Every book created was filled with about twenty pages of text on its subject, all of it written by members of the graphics department. These pages were repeated to fill up the book.

# THE TALES OF BEEDLE THE BARD

Because Hermione Granger inherits Dumbledore's copy of *The Tales of Beedle the Bard,* she later understands the importance of "The Tale of the Three Brothers," which tells the story of three wizard siblings who try to outsmart Death and end up receiving the Deathly Hallows—the Elder Wand, the Resurrection Stone, and the Cloak of Invisibility. Miraphora Mina and Eduardo Lima wanted to make the film's prop version of *The Tales of Beedle the Bard* extra special, so they embellished each tale with laser-cut illustrations that looked like delicate lace. The prop was so stunning that when J.K. Rowling saw it she asked to take the book home with her.

# Flourish and Blotts

Prop makers created a gravity-defying effect for the textbooks available at Flourish and Blotts bookshop in Diagon Alley in *Harry Potter and the Chamber of Secrets*, using a curved metal bar that went through a hole drilled into the middle of the books.

To create the menagerie of books seen in the films, the graphics department consulted with bookbinders to come up with ever more magical tomes. They made covers out of metal, silk, and gold leaf.

### Flying Off the Shelves

For the books to leap up to the library shelves at Hogwarts in *Harry Potter and the Half-Blood Prince,* set decorator Stephenie McMillan and her team made the book props out of lightweight material. Crew members wearing green gloves reached through the stacks to grasp the books, creating the illusion of flight once the green gloves were removed in post-production.

 Many of the books sitting on the shelves in Professor Dumbledore's office were actually phone books bound with fake covers.

# ◆ ◆ Wands ◆ ◆

A wand is an instrument used by a witch or wizard to channel their magical powers. As Garrick Ollivander says in *Harry Potter and the Sorcerer's Stone,* "The wand chooses the wizard." Since a wand selects the user who best matches its characteristics—and since no two wands are alike—many of the wands designed for the Harry Potter films were crafted with their owner in mind.

Ron's Taped Wand

Professor McGonagall's Wand

Professor Snape's Wand

HARRY POTTER & THE HALF-BLOOD PRINCE · ACTION PROP
PROFESSOR SLUGHORN'S WAND ~ DRAWN AT FULL SIZE
PLEASE READ WITH CONCEPT DRAWING. SEE ART DEPT. FOR EXACT FINISHES.

SILVER
STUDS

AS
WOOD

SILVER

SILVER 'SLUG TRAIL' PATTERN
CHASED INTO WOODEN SHAFT

END
ELEVA

SILVER

AS
WOOD

ELEVATION

Devon Murray, who plays student Seamus Finnigan, holds the record for breaking the most prop wands while filming a single scene: ten. However, over the course of the eight films, Daniel Radcliffe broke about eighty!

## The Real-Life Wand Makers

In the wizarding world, Ollivanders has been making fine wands since 382 BC. In the real world, wand making for the Harry Potter films began with the films' concept artists, who sketched out countless designs meant to capture a bit of each character's personality in the look of his or her wand. Once a design was decided upon, the prop-making team crafted a master copy of the wand on a thirteen- to fifteen-inch piece of wood. "We looked for interesting pieces of precious woods," prop maker Pierre Bohanna explains. "We chose wood that might have burrs or knots or interesting textures to create a unique shape to it." Once the wand was finalized, a mold was created so that the prop-making team could remake it in resin and make copies of the wands as needed.

### Harry's Wand

While Harry's wand in the first two films is quite simple, Daniel Radcliffe got to pick a new wand for *Harry Potter and the Prisoner of Azkaban.* Daniel picked a brown, gnarled-looking wand with a handle reminiscent of a tree trunk.

### Ron's Wand

Ron's first wand was also a simple design: it's thicker than most, almost like a baton, and scuffed. Since that wand is broken in *Harry Potter and the Chamber of Secrets* in an encounter with the Whomping Willow, Rupert Grint chose another wand the prop makers created. A bit similar to Harry's wand, it looks as if it was made from a whittled-down root.

◆

### Hermione's Wand

Hermione Granger's simple but elegant wand was hand-carved from a type of wood called "London plane" and then lightly stained to draw attention to the twisting, ivy-like growth that runs along it.

# Dark Wands

Concept artist Ben Dennett envisioned a variety of menacing-looking wands for use by Lord Voldemort's Death Eaters. These made prominent use of skulls and bones, Slytherinesque snake heads, and runes.

## It's All in the Family

Lucius Malfoy's wand has a sleek black shaft topped by an openmouthed snake head, which he keeps encased in his walking stick. When it came time to design Narcissa Malfoy's wand, concept artist Adam Brockbank sought to make a similar but more feminine version. "I took the same black wood that was used for Lucius's cane," Adam recalls.

The snake head on Lucius's wand has replaceable teeth, since these would often break when actor Jason Isaacs used the cane too roughly on set.

### Lord Voldemort's Wand

Concept artist Adam Brockbank imagined that Lord Voldemort's wand would have been carved from a human bone to resemble a "bony, evil finger." The wand handle looks like a human joint with a strange claw, and the rest of the wand is sharply tapered.

# QUIDDITCH GEAR

The wizarding sport of Quidditch is played with pride at Hogwarts. Played on broomsticks, the object of Quidditch is to score the most points by shooting a Quaffle through one of three hoops, or by catching the Golden Snitch. Teams are composed of seven players: three Chasers, who try to score goals with the Quaffle; two Beaters, who whack Bludger balls at the other team or away from their own; a Keeper, who guards the goal posts; and a Seeker, whose job it is to catch the Golden Snitch. Thanks to his natural broom-riding skills, Harry Potter becomes the youngest Seeker at Hogwarts in a century, according to his friend and teammate Ron Weasley.

### Quaffle

The Quaffle is a red leather ball that Chasers carry and pass to one another until they can attempt to throw it through one of three hoops. Described as twelve inches in diameter in J.K. Rowling's original novels, the Quaffle seen on film is a bit smaller—just nine inches in diameter. Stuart Craig sketched out several ideas for the Quaffle design, resulting in a red ball with indentations. Red leather was used to cover the prop Quaffle's foam core.

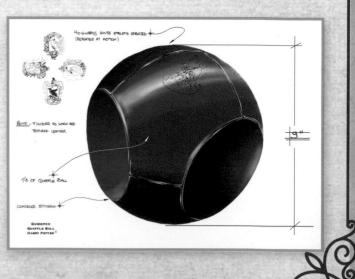

## Bludger

A Bludger is a heavy ball made of iron. Gryffindor captain Oliver Wood describes them as "nasty little buggers." The films' sound designers decided Bludgers should make a noise like an angry animal when hit with a Beater's bat.

## Beater's Bat

A variety of options was offered by production designer Stuart Craig for the magically strengthened wooden bats Beaters use to hit Bludgers, including a hand bat with a net laced between two prongs. Ultimately, the filmmakers decided on a simpler design.

# The Golden Snitch

The Golden Snitch is described as a walnut-size gold metallic ball with silver wings that help it fly around the Quidditch field at high speeds. Many different designs were considered for the film version of the Golden Snitch, including a version with mothlike wings, one with boat sails, and even one with fish fins. Eventually, the Golden Snitch prop had thin, ribbed wings in a smaller sail shape. The Golden Snitch ball itself was made with copper, then covered in gold.

### A Zipping Hummingbird

The visual effects team and sound department worked together to bring the Golden Snitch to life on-screen by making it fly and giving it a hummingbird-buzz sound as it whizzed by players' heads. The visual effects team paid careful attention to detail in making the Golden Snitch fly, even making a reflection of the Golden Snitch in Harry's glasses to keep the audience immersed.

# SAFETY FIRST

Quidditch players don all kinds of safety gear—from arm guards, called bays, designed to protect them from Bludgers, to leather body armor, helmets, and knee pads. Special rain gear and goggles were created for the actors to wear in *Harry Potter and the Prisoner of Azkaban* during the stormy Quidditch match.

# BROOMS

Not only are brooms an essential mode of transportation in the wizarding world, they're a cornerstone in the game of Quidditch. From the scraggly, crooked brooms that the first-year students learn to fly on in *Harry Potter and the Sorcerer's Stone* to the sleek brooms used by the Order in *Harry Potter and the Order of the Phoenix*, the prop-making team behind the Harry Potter films crafted many broomsticks, each more sophisticated than the last.

Concept artist Dermot Power created unusual textures for the Firebolt broom handle as well as various spell symbols for the broom's shaft in *Harry Potter and the Prisoner of Azkaban*.

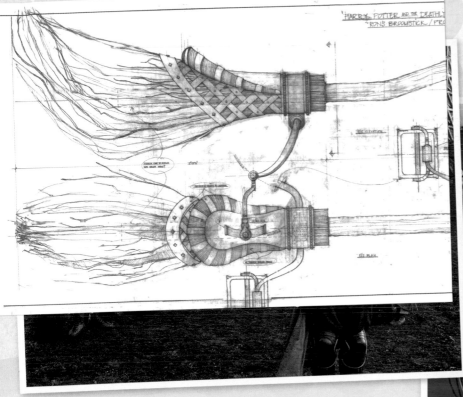

## Making Them Fly

To film broom-riding scenes, the actors would first put on harnesses, then sit strapped onto bicycle seats attached to their brooms. The brooms were mounted onto motion-control bases so that they could be easily twisted and turned in the air to imitate flying. The actors rode between eight or nine feet off the ground to as much as double that height. The complete flying effect wouldn't come together until the visual effects team had a chance to work with the shot footage.

## The Art of Broom Making

Harry receives a couple of brooms during his years at Hogwarts: a Nimbus 2000 from Professor McGonagall and a Firebolt from his godfather, Sirius Black. A world away from the worn-out brooms of Madam Hooch's class, the bristles on these are well-kept and the sticks far more aerodynamic. But the prop makers had to take into account much more than just the look of each broom: each needed to be light enough to be carried, but incredibly strong to survive filming, so airplane-grade titanium was used as a base. This was covered with mahogany wood. Birch branches were added for the bristles.

# Personalized Broomsticks

Quidditch moves fast, and the action-packed escape from number four, Privet Drive in *Harry Potter and the Order of the Phoenix* takes place at night, so it's not easy when watching the films to appreciate all the intricate details on each broom. Starting with *Harry Potter and the Prisoner of Azkaban*, concept artist Adam Brockbank and his team designed brooms to match the personalities of the riders.

Mad-Eye Moody got a motorcycle-style broomstick, while Remus Lupin's broom reflected his shabby appearance. Nymphadora Tonks's broom was built using different colored threads woven into the twigs of its bristle head to represent the ever-changing colors of the Metamorphmagus's hair. Viktor Krum, Durmstrang student and Seeker for the Bulgarian National Quidditch Team, rides a broom with a bright red broomstick.

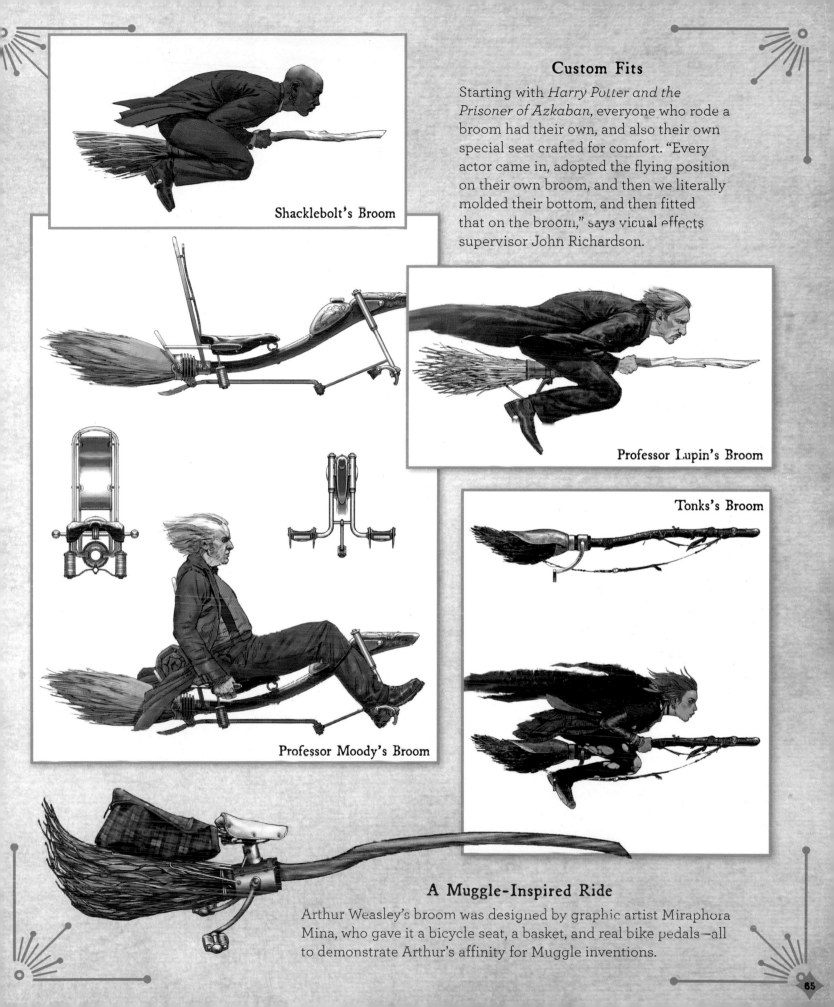

Shacklebolt's Broom

## Custom Fits

Starting with *Harry Potter and the Prisoner of Azkaban*, everyone who rode a broom had their own, and also their own special seat crafted for comfort. "Every actor came in, adopted the flying position on their own broom, and then we literally molded their bottom, and then fitted that on the broom," says visual effects supervisor John Richardson.

Professor Lupin's Broom

Tonks's Broom

Professor Moody's Broom

## A Muggle-Inspired Ride

Arthur Weasley's broom was designed by graphic artist Miraphora Mina, who gave it a bicycle seat, a basket, and real bike pedals—all to demonstrate Arthur's affinity for Muggle inventions.

# POTIONS

A bezoar is shoved down Ron Weasley's throat to save him from poisoned mead in *Harry Potter and the Half-Blood Prince*, essence of dittany is used by Hermione Granger to heal Ron's arm when he is splinched in *Harry Potter and the Deathly Hallows – Part 1*, and Polyjuice Potion is key to the plot of *Harry Potter and the Goblet of Fire*. Needless to say, an important part of being a witch or wizard is knowing one's way around potions and the ingredients that make them. For the Harry Potter films, the graphics department studiously created labels for potion supplies like Graphorn powder, armadillo bile, wormwood essence, and many others. These were applied to vials, bottles, and jars of all kinds, sourced by the props team, to dress the potions classroom and other sets.

### A Private Potions Collection

One of Professor Slughorn's most noted qualities in *Harry Potter and the Half-Blood Prince* is his desire to collect—both people, in the form of connections with notable students from the past and present, and things. So while in previous films the potions are assumed to be part of the Hogwarts stores and feature a range of styles, it made sense that many of the potion bottles seen in *Harry Potter and the Half-Blood Prince* would bear a particular phrase: "From the Apothecarium of Horace E. F. Slughorn."

If a scene required actors to drink potions straight from the bottles, carrot and coriander soup stood in for less tasty or fictional ingredients such as sliced caterpillar or dragon blood.

### Felix Felicis

In the book version of *Harry Potter and the Half-Blood Prince*, Felix Felicis (aka Liquid Luck) is described as looking like liquid gold, but in the film it's clear with a silvery hue. A specially designed vial was created by the art department for the Felix Felicis potion, complete with a miniature cauldron and an elaborate holding clamp.

Hundreds of potion labels were created by the graphics department, though many are barely, if at all, seen on-screen. For example, labels for "Restorative Potion" numbers 2 and 3 were created for Madame Maxime's personal medicine case, which is in the background during the second task of the Triwizard Tournament.

## Read the Label

In *Harry Potter and the Sorcerer's Stone*, the five hundred bottles in Professor Severus Snape's classroom were filled with all manner of items to stand in for potion ingredients: dried plants, animal bones collected from a butcher, and plastic animal toys from the London Zoo gift shop. The graphics department then made handwritten and handcrafted potion labels, which included serial numbers and lists of the ingredients. "Potion N. 07," for example, is said to contain "powdered bat wings" and "syrup of wild onion."

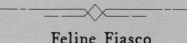

## Feline Fiasco

Polyjuice Potion allows the drinker to assume the physical appearance of another person, but sometimes drinking the potion can go terribly wrong. Concept art by Adam Brockbank envisions the scene when Hermione accidentally adds cat hair to her potion and winds up with a feline appearance.

# THE SORCERER'S STONE

In *Harry Potter and the Sorcerer's Stone,* Harry, Ron, and Hermione search for a magical object that is capable of producing the Elixir of Life, which is said to make the one who drinks it immortal. To keep Lord Voldemort from acquiring the Sorcerer's Stone, the Hogwarts professors hide it and place security obstacles to keep thieves at bay, including Fluffy, the giant three-headed dog; a temperamental tentacled plant called Devil's Snare; a locked door that only a winged key can open; a life-size game of chess that needs to be won before the player can move on; and the Mirror of Erised.

### Practical Plants

While Fluffy was created almost completely through special effects, the Devil's Snare plant was actually a very clever practical effect. Puppeteers placed below the plant slowly pulled off rubber vines that had been wrapped around the actors before shooting. Then the film was played backward so it appeared that the plant was entangling the characters instead of releasing them.

## Winged Keys

The design for the winged keys presented a unique challenge. "They had to be scary and wild, but not too scary or too wild," says visual effects supervisor Robert Legato. The keys were created digitally, with their movements modeled after the way a flock of birds flying together might suddenly change direction in the sky. One key wasn't generated digitally: used to open the door, this prop key featured wings made from iridescent silk.

## Chess Pieces

The final challenge involves a giant game of wizard chess. Large models of the thirty-two chess pieces were sculpted in clay and cast in various materials, with some of the pieces measuring up to twelve feet high and weighing up to five hundred pounds. The pieces were moved by radio controls. Each piece blew up after it was taken—an effect accomplished by using compressed air devices activated via remote control. "That was an incredible set," recalls actor Rupert Grint, "and such a cool scene, with pieces being smashed and exploding around us. I've still got a broken piece of the horse I was riding!"

## Mirror of Erised

This ancient mirror shows the "deepest, most desperate desire of our hearts." Running along the top of the mirror is the quote "Erised stra ehru oyt ube cafru oyt on wohsi," which reversed says "I show not your face but your heart's desire." Only one version of the Mirror of Erised prop was constructed for the film. Fortunately, it never broke.

### The Sorcerer's Stone

J.K. Rowling described the Sorcerer's Stone as looking like an uncut ruby, but when several prop stones were created out of plastic for the film, they looked more like a huge piece of hard candy. In order to give it the flickering effect of a real gem, filmmakers got creative with the lighting and used a small flame placed on top of the camera that was reflected in red plastic.

# THE TRIWIZARD TOURNAMENT

The three largest wizarding schools in Europe—Hogwarts School of Witchcraft and Wizardry, Beauxbatons Academy of Magic, and Durmstrang Institute—hold a dangerous competition, the Triwizard Tournament, where a chosen student from each school competes in three tasks that test their courage, cunning, and magical talents.

Harry Potter

Cedric Diggory

Fleur Delacour

Viktor Krum

## The Goblet of Fire

Any student wishing to volunteer for the Triwizard Tournament must write their name on a piece of parchment and throw it into the flame in the Goblet of Fire. While production designer Stuart Craig originally conceived the Goblet of Fire as being a small, bejeweled metal cup, this quickly changed. The goblet we see on film is an interesting mix of natural and more magical elements: the bottom part is made up of rugged timber from an English elm tree that creeps up to meet the base of the goblet. This design helped lend the goblet its mystery, as if it's a living thing.

# The Golden Egg

For the first challenge of the Triwizard Tournament, the champions must steal a golden egg from a very protective and dangerous dragon. If the champion succeeds, he or she must open the egg to receive a special clue as to the nature of the next challenge that awaits.

Miraphora Mina was inspired by the decorative and highly collectible Fabergé eggs, which were originally created for the Russian imperial family in the 1880s.

### Springing into Action

The golden egg in the film has the etched design of a city on the outside and is a bit of a puzzle to open. "I wanted something that would spring open automatically," Miraphora Mina says, "but only if you had the right code." She designed the device as a little owl's head that sits atop six feathers. Once the top is turned, the gold-plated sides of the egg open out like three wings—a nod to the three tasks of the Triwizard Tournament.

### What's Inside?

The core of the egg is made up of a resin solution with small acrylic balls and pigments swirling inside, which makes it look as if there's a moving current inside the egg. "In a way, it looks as though it's actually alive inside," notes Miraphora.

# TRIWIZARD TOURNAMENT CUP

The winning student is presented with the chalice of champions, the vessel of victory, the highly decorative Triwizard Cup. The number three is key to the Triwizard Tournament—the tournament is made up of three tasks, with three wizarding schools competing—so there are nods to that everywhere in the cup's design: three twisting dragons form the handles of the cup, with the word TRI-WIZ-ARD broken into thirds, one on each side of the front panels.

## A Heavy Look

When it came time to create the cup from Miraphora Mina's design, prop maker Pierre Bohanna knew he didn't want to use silver. "We wanted it to look like it was a weighty casting, and a very old piece." By combining metal alloys, Pierre was able to achieve a lead-like finish. Once completed, a mold of each piece of the cup was created so that different versions could be made for other scenes. Some were made in latex and others in rubber, which were used to send the prop flying when it's used as a Portkey.

A Portkey is an object that is enchanted in order to instantly transport anyone who touches it to a specific place.

# HORCRUXES

A Horcrux is an object or person into which a witch or a wizard has placed a fragment of their soul, allowing them to live even if their body is destroyed. Creating Horcruxes is a very Dark form of magic; Horcruxes can only be created by committing murder. In pursuit of immortality, Lord Voldemort hides part of his soul in seven Horcruxes and places them in hiding places. Harry Potter makes it his mission to find and destroy all seven in order to rid the world of Voldemort once and for all.

## TOM RIDDLE'S DIARY

Lord Voldemort entrusts his first Horcrux—Tom Riddle's diary—to Death Eater Lucius Malfoy, who later slips it to Ginny Weasley without her knowing. Its magical power possesses Ginny, compelling her to re-open the Chamber of Secrets. Eventually, Harry Potter finds the diary and uses a Basilisk fang to destroy it.

### Stages of Destruction

In *Harry Potter and the Chamber of Secrets*, the leather journal starts out with just a few scratches, but as it passes from owner to new owner, the diary suffers water damage (when Ginny tries to flush it down the toilet) and then ultimately spews black fluid when pierced by a Basilisk fang. The Basilisk fang used in the film to destroy the diary was made from rubber and designed not to hurt if you accidentally stabbed yourself with it.

TOM MARVOLO RIDDLE

# MARVOLO GAUNT'S RING

Passed down for generations in Voldemort's family, this ring's original owner was Salazar Slytherin. In a nod to its Slytherin origins, graphic artist Miraphora Mina designed the ring to feature two stylized snake heads that meet to hold the black Resurrection Stone in their jaws. Two versions of the ring were created by the prop makers: a small version to fit the young Tom Riddle and a larger version with a cracked stone for Professor Dumbledore, who eventually destroys the Horcrux using the Sword of Gryffindor.

## Salazar Slytherin's Locket

Salazar Slytherin's locket is converted into a Horcrux that influences those who wear it in negative and powerful ways. Originally, the locket is hidden in the Crystal Cave, but it eventually ends up with Dolores Umbridge, who receives it as a bribe. Ron Weasley destroys the locket with the Sword of Gryffindor.

The movie prop locket is made of gold and features a serpentine *S* in glittering green stones on the front. The locket's face is overlaid with astrological symbols that refer to the relative angles of planets to one another. "The locket was a challenge because it was full of evil, but it also needed to have a beauty to it: to be something appealing and something historical," says Miraphora Mina.

### The Real Thing

Miraphora designed two lockets: a crude version to represent the fake locket left by Sirius Black's brother, Regulus, in the Crystal Cave, and a more elegant version for the real thing. The real locket's design was inspired by an eighteenth-century jewelry piece from Spain that Miraphora saw in a museum. Miraphora drafted a number of different versions until she got the Slytherin locket exactly right.

# HELGA HUFFLEPUFF'S CUP

Created by one of the founders of Hogwarts, this magical golden cup has two finely wrought handles and features the Hufflepuff house symbol—a badger—engraved on the side. Converted into a Horcrux by Lord Voldemort, it is later entrusted to Bellatrix Lestrange and hidden away in the Lestrange family vault at Gringotts. There it is protected by a spell: anything touched in the vault multiplies in number. Eventually, Hermione Granger destroys the cup in the Chamber of Secrets using a Basilisk fang.

### Thousands of Cups

When Miraphora Mina began designing Helga Hufflepuff's cup, J.K. Rowling's novel *Harry Potter and the Deathly Hallows* hadn't been released. The filmmakers originally wanted the cup to be in the Room of Requirement in *Harry Potter and the Half-Blood Prince*, but its first time on-screen was in the final film in the series. "I can't say whether it would have affected the design if we had known that it was going to need to multiply into thousands and thousands," recalls Miraphora, who was inspired by medieval goblets in her design. The prop-making team ended up making soft rubber copies of six different objects, including the Hufflepuff cup, to make enough treasure to fill twenty cubic meters of the vault.

# Rowena Ravenclaw's Diadem

Once belonging to Rowena Ravenclaw, this diadem (an ornate tiara) is inscribed with Ravenclaw's famous phrase, "Wit beyond measure is man's greatest treasure." Harry locates the diadem hidden in the Room of Requirement. After narrowly escaping Fiendfyre accidentally set off in the room by Slytherin Gregory Goyle, Harry stabs it with a Basilisk fang before Ron kicks it into the flames.

Designed by concept artist Adam Brockbank, the diadem's design evokes the Ravenclaw eagle. The eagle's wings are outlined in white gems, and its body and tail feathers are enhanced with three multifaceted pale blue stones.

# Nagini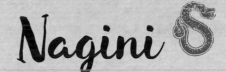

The snake Nagini makes for a horrifying Horcrux that never leaves Lord Voldemort's side. While Nagini is a very powerful enemy, Neville Longbottom manages to behead the serpent with the Sword of Gryffindor during the Battle of Hogwarts. Nagini's design was inspired by a mix of Burmese python and anaconda, though viper- and cobra-like movements were added later. The film's creature shop created a fully painted maquette (model) of the snake at her full size of twenty feet, which was then digitally scanned for computer animators to enhance.

# HARRY POTTER

After killing James and Lily Potter, Voldemort attempts to murder baby Harry. When the Killing Curse Voldemort casts at him rebounds, it leaves a lightning-bolt-shaped scar on Harry's forehead—and has the unintended effect of making him a Horcrux. The part of Voldemort's soul that resides in Harry is destroyed during the Battle of Hogwarts when Voldemort casts the Killing Curse at Harry again.

# THE DEATHLY HALLOWS

The Deathly Hallows are three very powerful magical objects—the Elder Wand, the Resurrection Stone, and the Cloak of Invisibility—that allow the owner of all three to become the Master of Death. Raised as a Muggle, Harry never read "The Tale of the Three Brothers" when he was young. If he'd known the story, he might not have asked about the strange-looking necklace worn by Luna Lovegood's father, Xenophilius, at Bill Weasley's wedding in *Harry Potter and the Deathly Hallows – Part 1*. Little does Harry know then that the three objects symbolized in the necklace will be key to defeating Lord Voldemort.

### The Symbol of the Hallows

The Deathly Hallows are symbolized by a circle split by a line encased within a triangle. The circle is for the Resurrection Stone, which can bring loved ones back from the dead. The triangle represents the Cloak of Invisibility. The line in the center symbolizes the Elder Wand, the most powerful wand in existence. Miraphora Mina designed the golden necklace worn by Xenophilius Lovegood.

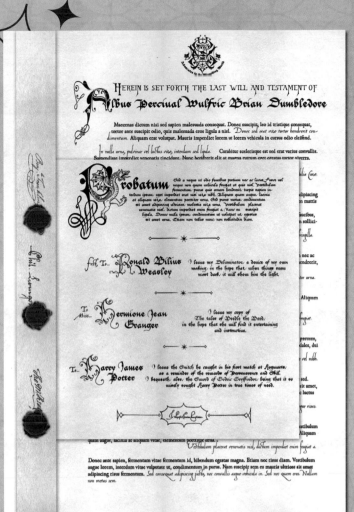

## Albus Dumbledore's Will

Professor Dumbledore's will is read to Harry, Ron, and Hermione by Minister for Magic Rufus Scrimgeour in *Harry Potter and the Deathly Hallows - Part 1*. In it, Dumbledore bequeaths one of the Deathly Hallows—the Resurrection Stone, hidden in the Golden Snitch—to Harry. A clue to the Hallows' existence in the form of his copy of *The Tales of Beedle the Bard* goes to Hermione, and the Deluminator is left to Ron. The will was created by the graphics department, who stained and aged the parchment and affixed it with several wax seals.

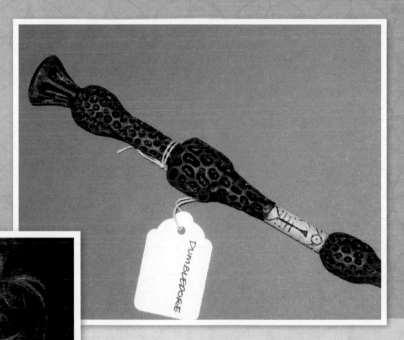

## The Elder Wand

When the prop makers created Professor Dumbledore's wand for *Harry Potter and the Sorcerer's Stone*, they had no idea the wand would be so central to the story. The wand was carved from English oak and inlaid near the handle with a white, bone-like material inscribed with runes. One of the thinnest wands created for the Harry Potter films, it features honeycombed nodules every two or three inches, making it very easy to spot at a distance.

# THE RESURRECTION STONE

Both a Horcrux and a Hallow, the Resurrection Stone was given by Death to the second brother who wanted to bring back his bride from the dead. But it only serves to bring back a shade of the dead, not a living, breathing body. The stone eventually found its way to Tom Riddle, who turned it into a Horcrux after murdering his grandfather.

## Mysterious Bling

Designing the Resurrection Stone—which in *Harry Potter and the Half-Blood Prince* was described only as a gemmed ring for Dumbledore—was tricky for the props team since they didn't yet know how important it would be later in the films. "We were as much in the dark as everyone else when we first started designing the stone for the ring Dumbledore had in the sixth film," art director Hattie Storey recalls. When the novel *Harry Potter and the Deathly Hallows* came out, "I read through it in a real hurry, and what we learned changed our ideas for the stone."

# The Cloak of Invisibility

In *Harry Potter and the Sorcerer's Stone*, Harry receives an Invisibility Cloak for Christmas with a mysterious note saying the cloak originally belonged to his father, James Potter. It isn't until the final film that Harry discovers the cloak's origin and the consequence of its being one of the Deathly Hallows.

## The Visible Cloak

While the original novel describes the cloak as being made from a "shining, silvery cloth," costume designer Judianna Makovsky used a lush velvet fabric that was dyed and imprinted with astrological, Celtic, and runic symbols to create the prop used for the film.

# 73 P
INV. C

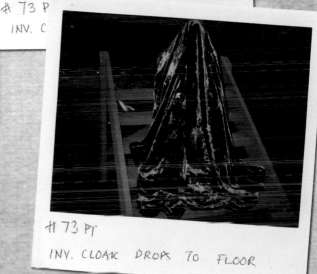

# 73 PT
INV. CLOAK DROPS TO FLOOR

## Disappearing On-Screen

Actor Daniel Radcliffe used a version of the cloak lined with green-screen material. By flipping the cloak inside out, only the green-screen fabric would be visible—making it easy for the special effects teams to edit out the green and, with a bit of movie magic, give the effect of total invisibility.

# PENSIEVE AND MEMORY CABINET

The Pensieve is a shallow basin that allows a viewer to see memories siphoned from a wizard's mind. Harry accidentally discovers the Pensieve in *Harry Potter and the Goblet of Fire*, when he enters into Professor Dumbledore's memories of Karkaroff and Barty Crouch Jr. at the Death Eater trials. The Pensieve is later used in *Harry Potter and the Half-Blood Prince*, where Harry is able to view a conversation between Professor Slughorn and Tom Riddle about Horcruxes, and in *Harry Potter and the Deathly Hallows – Part 2*, where Harry learns Professor Snape's true nature.

## Inky Memories

Digital artists created a computer-generated liquid surface for the Pensieve that included realistic ripples and waves for *Harry Potter and the Goblet of Fire*. The artists also included threads of silver-looking fluid that would swirl and eddy around the shallow basin before dissolving into the memory. For *Harry Potter and the Half Blood Prince*, the memory introduced into the Pensieve takes the shape of inky black threads instead.

## Memory Cabinet Contents

The memories used in the Pensieve are stored in small vials created by prop maker Pierre Bohanna, with handwritten labels carefully made by the graphics department. More than eight hundred vials were placed in Professor Dumbledore's golden memory cabinet.

# Weasleys' Wizard Wheezes

Fred and George Weasley's Diagon Alley joke shop, Weasleys' Wizard Wheezes, sells practical jokes, candy, potions, and more, including fake wands and Extendable Ears. "You can buy all different types of pranks, but there's some good remedies mixed in as well," explains Oliver Phelps, who plays George Weasley. "Things like the Ten-Second Pimple Vanisher cream would actually make a fortune if they sold it to Muggles." The Weasley twins had a small-scale business at Hogwarts selling their products, but their storefront in *Harry Potter and the Half-Blood Prince* took them to a whole new level.

## Unlimited Wares

Nosebleed Nougats, Fever Fudge, Fainting Fancies, Decoy Detonators, edible Dark Marks, and even a toy version of Arthur Weasley's flying Ford Anglia line the shelves of the Weasleys' Wizard Wheezes set. "There were so many layers of props in the store," notes props art director Hattie Storey, "that we ended up making *too many* props." The brief scene shown at the start of *Harry Potter and the Half-Blood Prince* couldn't do justice to the enormous amount of wares designed and crafted. "We didn't know which ones the director would feature, so we kind of did everything," Hattie says. Blueprints for everything from Decoy Detonators to Fanged Frisbees had to be put together to show exactly how each prop would be constructed.

Weasleys' Wizard Wheezes was stocked with an estimated forty thousand products.

# WHEEZE-LY GRAPHICS

Not only did the toys and candies have to be designed, but so did the packaging. "This was really a designer's dream," says graphic artist Miraphora Mina. "To be told you have to design every single package for a four-story shop of magical jokes owned by two teenagers who probably don't have much of a design sense. We had to throw away all our ideas of good design and use clashing colors and dreadful printing techniques." The graphics department found their inspiration in the packaging for cheap fireworks and firecrackers.

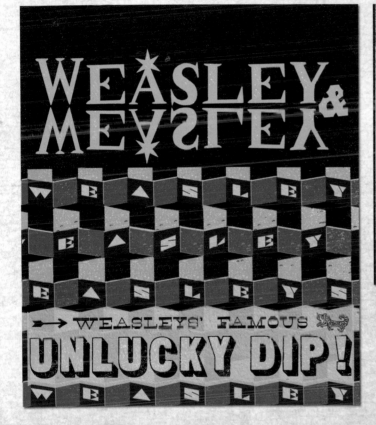

### Gingerly Decorated

Most shops have some kind of window dressing. "But Fred and George do one better," explains James Phelps, who plays Fred Weasley. "It's not really like your average five-foot mannequin," adds Oliver Phelps, referring to the large Weasley twin adorning the outside of the shop. "It's probably about twenty feet high." The Weasley colors are prominent inside the shop as well. "The whole shop is ginger, pretty much," remarks Oliver Phelps, "like the Weasleys with their bright orange hair."

# WIZARDING INVENTIONS

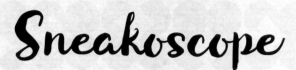

## Sneakoscope

Resembling a glass toy top, the Sneakoscope is an invention that whistles if Dark or untrustworthy magic is happening nearby. In a deleted scene from *Harry Potter and the Prisoner of Azkaban*, Ron Weasley buys a Sneakoscope for Harry from Dervish and Banges to cheer up his friend, who wasn't able to join his classmates at Hogsmeade. Later, in *Harry Potter and the Half-Blood Prince*, the Sneakoscope appears on the shelves of Weasleys' Wizard Wheezes.

### A Dozen Designs

More than a dozen possible designs were sketched out by concept artist Dermot Power for the Sneakoscope, from metallic versions to a more severe-looking black-and-red option. Dermot specified which materials should be used by the prop makers and included descriptions of how to use the top as well.

# HOWLER

This magical letter arrives in a red envelope and delivers the written message in the writer's voice, often at a loud volume, hence the name Howler. What happens if you just ignore the letter, you might ask? Well, let's just say it's best to get it over with. In *Harry Potter and the Chamber of Secrets*, Ron Weasley receives a Howler from his upset mother, Molly, who scolds him for stealing his father's enchanted car and driving it to Hogwarts.

## A Screaming Envelope

The Howler seen on film is inspired by origami, the Japanese art of folding paper. Through a series of clever folds, the seemingly innocent ribbon-wrapped envelope becomes a harsh red mouth with the ribbon for a tongue, and the letter's white paper held inside becomes a full set of teeth. To make it appear as if the Howler was actually speaking, shapes that mimicked a human mouth reciting the dialogue were created as reference.

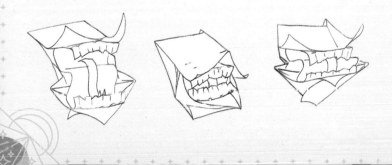

# THE FLYING FORD ANGLIA

Arthur Weasley's Ford Anglia is special—it's enchanted, enabling it to fly and become invisible. Ron Weasley and Harry Potter drive the out-of-control flying Ford Anglia over London in *Harry Potter and the Chamber of Secrets*, making a crash landing outside Hogwarts in the Whomping Willow. Though vehicles are not always considered props, the flying Ford Anglia is a wizarding invention beloved by fans.

## Car Collectors

The type of Ford Anglia seen on-screen isn't exactly a popular model these days. To acquire enough for use for filming, visual effects supervisor John Richardson and his crew had to scour England for more than a dozen Anglias. "We needed fourteen cars, to be used in various stages, from mint condition when the boys first steal the car and rescue Harry, through to the landing in the tree, and finally to going wild in the Forbidden Forest," explains Richardson. Thankfully, most of the Ford Anglias used in the film weren't in great condition to begin with and were headed for the junkyard, so it wasn't as though they were destroying valuable vintage cars.

# The Weasleys' Clocks

When Harry Potter first visits the Weasley family home, The Burrow, he is in awe of the different clocks the family owns. Amazingly, the clocks don't tell time, but rather all kinds of other things. Designed by concept artist Cyrille Nomberg, the wooden clock that hangs in the kitchen features chore reminders like "Call the Ministry," "Darn Robes," "Clean Ron's Owl," and "Check for Boggarts."

### The Grandfather Clock

Also in the house stands a colorful grandfather clock that shows where all the members of the family are at the time—home, work, school, or in trouble. The hands on the vintage clock were made from scissor handles with green-screen material in the handles that was later replaced in post-production with film footage of the actors' faces. "It's my favorite prop from all the films," says Daniel Radcliffe. "It shows where the Weasleys are and what's happening to them, even if they're in mortal peril."

# THE DELUMINATOR

Left to Ron Weasley in Professor Dumbledore's will, the Deluminator (known as the Put-Outer in *Harry Potter and the Sorcerer's Stone*) is a mechanical device that is able to draw in light from a nearby source. With the flip of a switch, it can also reverse the effect and release the light back to its source.

The Deluminator is covered in malachite, a green semiprecious stone.

## How Would a Deluminator Work?

It was up to art director Hattie Storey to construct a blueprint and demonstrate how the clever device would work. Hattie's designs show a small tool with caps on either end. One of the caps would flip up and back when a switch on the side is moved, triggering a small piece to shoot up the top. From there, another even smaller piece pops up that takes in or releases light.

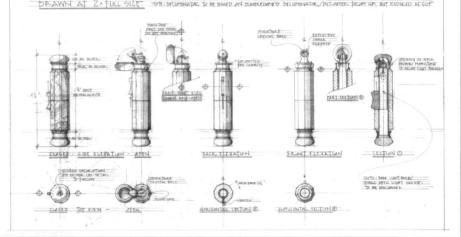

## Let the Light Guide You

Who could have known that the small tool Professor Dumbledore uses to turn out the streetlights at the start of *Harry Potter and the Sorcerer's Stone* would turn out to be so important to Harry Potter's story? In *Harry Potter and the Deathly Hallows – Part 1*, Ron is able to use the Deluminator to find his wandering friends after leaving them following an argument. When he clicks it on, a tiny ball of light appears, then enters his chest, and Ron knows it will lead him back to Harry and Hermione.

# THE TIME-TURNER

Hermione Granger has a very ambitious class schedule during her third year at Hogwarts. In fact, she is taking so many classes that it's only possible for her to attend all of them through the use of a time-travel device—the Time-Turner. Designed by Miraphora Mina, the Time-Turner prop is a golden piece of jewelry inspired by astrological instruments like astrolabes. When not in use, it lies flat. "But when she uses it," remarks Miraphora, "it comes alive, it becomes 3-D because it's really a ring within a ring that opens up to allow part of it to spin."

## Poetic Engravings

Miraphora Mina had two mottos engraved onto the Time-Turner prop. The outside ring reads, "I mark the hours every one, nor have I yet outrun the sun." The inside ring reads, "My use and value unto you depends on what you have to do."

## Hourglass Designs

Concept artist Dermot Power explored a variety of designs for the Time-Turner, making frequent use of an hourglass-shaped element that would spin and turn within clocks, vials, and pendants.

# Make Your Own Wand!

## WHAT YOU NEED:

- Pair of disposable wooden chopsticks
- Air-dry clay
- Paper clip
- Craft paint (acrylic)
- Craft paint brush

## INSTRUCTIONS:

1. Wrap a chunk of clay around the thick end of one of the chopsticks. It should start at about the middle of the stick and wrap around the end to make a rounded handle.

2. You can pick out a wand from the films to make, or you can create your own. If you want your wand to match one described in this book, turn to that page for reference. To make Hermione's wand, it is best to break off another piece of clay and roll it into a long strand. Wrap the long strand around the chopstick wand to make the vine. You can also pinch off extra small pieces of clay to make smaller vines and add these along the main vine.

3. Use the end of the extra chopstick to smooth and mold the clay.

4. Straighten out one end of the paper clip.

5. Use the paper clip's straightened end and the point of the extra chopstick to add texture to your wand. For wood grain, draw lines with the end of the paper clip. For pockmarks, poke the paper clip end or chopstick end into the clay.

6. Lay your wand on a smooth, dry surface, like wax paper. Let it dry for at least twenty-four hours.

7. When it is dry, paint the whole wand—both clay and chopstick—in a solid color.

8. Optional: Paint details on your wand with darker and lighter colors.

First U.S. edition 2017

ISBN 978-0-7636-9584-2

Published by
Candlewick Press
99 Dover Street
Somerville, Massachusetts 02144

visit us at www.candlewick.com

Produced by

INSIGHT
EDITIONS
PO Box 3088
San Rafael, CA 94912
www.insighteditions.com

Publisher: Raoul Goff
Associate Publisher: Vanessa Lopez
Art Director: Chrissy Kwasnik
Designer: Leah Bloise
Project Editor: Greg Solano
Managing Editor: Alan Kaplan
Production Editor: Rachel Anderson
Production Managers: Thomas Chung, Alix Nicholaeff, and Lina sp Temena

REPLANTED PAPER

Insight Editions, in association with Roots of Peace, will plant two trees for each tree
used in the manufacturing of this book. Roots of Peace is an internationally renowned
humanitarian organization dedicated to eradicating land mines worldwide and
converting war-torn lands into productive farms and wildlife habitats. Roots of Peace
will plant two million fruit and nut trees in Afghanistan and provide farmers there with
the skills and support necessary for sustainable land use.

Manufactured in Shenzhen, China, by Insight Editions

20175842R0
17 18 19 20 21 22 HHO 10 9 8 7 6 5 4 3 2 1